HELLO NIGHT!

HEALING THOUGHTS
FOR SLEEPLESS NIGHTS

HERBERT BROKERING

Augsburg
MINNEAPOLIS

Hello, Night! is dedicated to
night shadows, full moons, falling stars,
and times together with God in the dark.

HELLO, NIGHT!
Healing Thoughts for Sleepless Nights

Cover image courtesy of Clip Shots Stock Photography. Used by permission.
Cover design by Mike Mihelich.
Book design by Timothy W. Larson.

Library of Congress Cataloging in Publication Data
Brokering, Herbert F.
  Hello, night! : healing thoughts for sleepless nights / by Herbert Brokering.
  p. cm.
ISBN 0-8066-3837-0
  1. Insomniacs—Prayer-books and devotions—English. I. Title.
BV4910.4.B76 1999
242—dc21
                                                98-43673
                                                  CIP

Manufactured in the U.S.A.   AF 9-3837

03   02   01   00   99   1   2   3   4   5   6   7   8   9   10

HELLO
NIGHT!

Contents

FOREWORD
Hello, Night Reader!

This book is about making friends with night. When nighttime is my friend, I welcome it with the greeting: "Hello, Night!"

Through the years, illness and major surgery have made my nights special. I have learned to live with the waking hours. I have learned to know night in short and long spans of time. Seldom do I sleep more than four hours without waking. Sometimes I nap through the night. I add the naps, and when they total five or six hours, I call it a night.

I have faced different parts of night and made each my friend. Night has as many segments, rhythms, cycles as does day. It has seasons—winter, summer, autumn, springtime—as does a year. There is the waking, the moment after the waking. There is the fear, the worry, the anxious time. And there is the breaking through of a dream, a hope, a wish, a new idea.

Night is a quiet time for self-examination, for a close look at a big thought, a large worry, a great plan, a vision. Few interruptions disturb night thoughts. In a waking moment I stand before a mirror, see myself, hear my cries, sense my spirit, know my love, test my trust.

In a sudden waking, I meet God with worry or anger or stress or suspense. My night thoughts are prayers. They are felt, imagined, wished, asked, confessed inside the mind of God. They are thoughts inside thoughts greater than my own, part of a great whole. My night thoughts sense God's holiness, God's healing wholeness. And my prayers turn to love, adoration, faith, thanks. Night visions and dreams, clouds and darkness, still small voices in midnight caves—these have been holy ground in spiritual stories. Nighttime can be holy ground for us, too.

In the night I also meet myself when I was little. I woke in the night sixty years ago and had deep thoughts about God, myself, others. I started waking when little and began learning what is hurtful, helpful, possible at night. Now I meet young Herbert in the darkness and tell him what I know, what I have learned.

Hello, Night! is what I have learned. The fifty thoughts for sleepless nights are spiritual medicine for healing, growing, resting. They are night letters from me to you. The letters are my experiences through six decades. I know each problem, each solution. I know the hurt, the wake, the worry, the joy, the excitement; and I know the peace, the sleep. I know the medicine that worked for me.

Hello, Night! is not meant to cover night wounds with a little tape. It may not replace a sleep clinic or a doctor. It is meant to follow sleepless-night pain to its source, to heal a night wound from inside out. Healing can happen in the night—any night, even a sleepless night. Healing thoughts can shape the nighttime spirit, body, mind. Worries and fears that waken can be healed. Perhaps not removed, but healed.

To sleep through the night is no longer my goal. Nighttime is for me a journey of sleep and wakefulness. At times it is a wonderful journey, at times it is still a struggle. I need old and new healing thoughts. No nighttime exercise of mine is finished. The fifty healing thoughts in *Hello, Night!* have helped me. Some I have used once, some a hundred times. They repeat, they are continuous.

I keep discovering new faces of night, wakeful sides of darkness in which I am growing to be unafraid, hopeful, content, rested, glad. *Hello, Night!* is written that you, too, may grow healthy toward night and daytime alike.

Read the book when you get ready for bed, or open it when you wake during the night. Read one entire thought, or one line in a thought. At the end of each thought is a small prayer—healing words to focus your thoughts, to aim at God. The prayers bring me comfort when I say them over and over to myself, aloud and silently. Try them yourself.

I wish you a friendly night!

Herbert Brokering

Herbert Brokering
Minneapolis, Minnesota

It's the Room, the Clock, the Bed

O God, open my eyes in the dark.

I KEEP WAKING UP.

I wake in the night. Is it worry that wakens me? Why do I wake again and again? Fear of waking becomes my worry. And then, alas, nighttime—bedtime—worries me.

Two hours of sleep, and now I'm awake. I want sleep to be my friend. But waking time? What is there to do in the dark, when I wish I were asleep?

Whenever I wake at night—2 A.M. or 4 A.M.—I use this time in the dark to practice resting, deep breathing, remembering, praying. I make peace with being awake. I refresh my spirit.

I enjoy a single thought, a blessing, the voice of a friend, family, a memory. I liked dark places when I was a child. It's where we hid, where we were found during games of hide-and-seek. In the dark I find treasures. I find what I cherish, like apples and pears we wrapped in newspaper and saved through winter in a dark cellar. The aroma of the dark cellar is with me on my night watch.

When I wake I have a quiet time to pray. I pray for friends across the world who are already into tomorrow, hours ahead. In the dark, I am with them in their daytime—in Warsaw, Berlin, Slovakia, Tokyo.

In the dark I hear my neighbor go to work, a lover come home, travelers in planes overhead. And I may fall asleep enjoying a new thought, a prayer.

I remember when I slept through nights. What did I miss? How did I know night then? Did I see stars fall, watch long night shadows, see clouds roll over a harvest moon?

The florescent face of the night clock is becoming a friend. Two more hours of sleep. Thank you. Two and two is four hours. Almost enough for the night. Night time is like a game. I add up the score; each inning counts. Sometimes I strike out. Sometimes I hit a home run. Last night I slept three hours without waking. Total: seven hours.

In the morning I know I how long I slept; I know when I woke. I remember good thoughts in the dark, stars I saw, people remembered, love felt, rest gained. To wake at different times in the dark is like having different times in a day.

As child I learned a prayer for waking. It begins, "How gladly I have waked this morn." Last night I woke three times, three times I prayed, "How gladly I have waked." Little prayers of thanks. Keeping score, winning in the morning.

Waking has become a gift. It is a little resurrection in the night. When I add the sleeping and waking hours of a night, night becomes a friend. I give thanks, I take the new day.

Night wakings bring the world close to me.

I CAN'T SLEEP IN THIS ROOM.

Sometimes a room won't let me sleep.

When I wake suddenly, disturbed, the room feels too wide awake. Sometimes my bedroom fills with thoughts of worry and stress. I toss and turn; my resting place is no longer restful. I may need to find another place to sleep.

A friend was called to minister in a large church. The building was elegant, beautiful; but recently it had been filled with much parish pain and stress. The new minister opened all the windows for a day and announced a cleansing. Sun shone in, wind blew through all the rooms. Wind, spirit, breath—these are the same word in Scriptures. The church was blown clean.

My neighbor is a nurse. I told her about my sleeping problems, and she said, "A room can sometimes be filled with worry. Leave the room for a night; leave the problems behind. Take your pillow and go to another room or to a comfortable chair—someplace else to sleep."

Sometimes I sleep in two rooms during a single night. There is a couch I like in a room I seldom use. And there is a reclining chair where I rest by a window, where sleep returns. At the north end of our house is a room with many windows. In the night, this room shows me tree shadows. It shows me stars, the moon, the Big Dipper, a whole universe. Open sky makes for a restful place. Mother Nature holds me close, quiets me, brings sleep.

I have other sleeping places, too, places from childhood which live deep inside me: a hayloft, a tree house, a sleeping bag, atop a warm cellar door under the south sun, a couch near a wood stove, a spot of rug beside my dog. I remember sleeping on a country church bench during evening worship. Best of all was the corner of the back seat in our '28 Chevy, riding home in the dark.

Childhood places can be recalled; I can go to these places on restless nights, I can sleep there.

And I can borrow good sleeping places from the Bible. I can sleep at the rock of safety and blessing where Jacob saw angels ascending and descending. I can rest behind the temple altar where Samuel slept as a child. I can sleep in green pastures, beside the still waters of Psalm 23. Or I like the inn of Bethlehem, snuggling at the edge of the nativity, a safe corner in a quiet cave.

There are safe places for rest and sleep.

I am in a safe place.

I'm not ready for sleep.

More light can set my sleep clock back.

Light affects sleep and wake cycles in us. The sleep timer in us is exacting. On dark days, in overcast seasons, nighttime and sleep seem to come sooner. Light postpones feelings of sleepiness.

There are ways to open and close day. There are ways to open and close night. A doctor told me how to sleep and how to wake. Wake as a cat will waken: stretch, yawn, meet the day slowly. It is the same with night. Do not hurry into night, do not shut down day too soon. Stay in daylight or light until the night comes.

Where will I find this light? How can I expose myself to outdoor light in late afternoon and early evening?

In late afternoons and evenings, sit by a window. Watch the sunset, see daylight to the end. Keep shades and curtains open longer. Finish work or reading under a bright light. Extra time in light can keep me active one more hour. This waking hour can give me a better sleep.

I am learning not to hurry nighttime. Sometimes we need more light before entering night. We are children of light.

When I was little, we had no electric light. We did not hurry the night. Farm folks used nature's light to the end. We stayed with daytime into dusk and were there for each sunset. Night came slowly. Chairs and tables were set by windows. We cherished light of any kind. Kerosene and gas lanterns were lighted when night was dark. A dim lantern kept a ray of sunlight in my country bedroom.

Postponing night can give me a longer night rest. The end of daylight gets us ready for sleep.

Day is done. I am ready to sleep.

Herbert Brokering

My body clock isn't working.

I have a clock inside me. Years ago, when I needed to sleep, I often began writing projects. I stayed at the table sleeping and waking, working when my body was telling me to rest. I woke early and began while the family was still asleep. Nights were brief.

I am a morning person, but I lived as a night person. It did not fit. I ignored the clock keeping time inside myself. I was productive, but I was hard on myself, hard on others.

My doctor told me about night and day persons. My body has its own cycles of sleep and wake. It has its own rhythms. It is helpful for me to understand this part of myself.

Sleep is sacred. Miracles happen during sleep. Sacred times have rituals, routines, rules. The bedroom is for sleep. The bedroom is not for watching TV, balancing a checkbook, writing stories. The bedroom has its own agenda; it is for rest.

I am learning other sleep rules. Relax before bedtime. Avoid debates and grandiose planning. Relax before sleep.

Preparation for sleep has rituals that give me security. Shower, dress for bed, set the clock, position the pillows, read briefly, pray—all are part of my routine. We all have routines. Preparation for sleep also includes feelings toward others, showing love, speaking a goodnight word.

Body rhythms and cycles are designed for our well being. They are medicine in us. Learn to know your sleep cycles, learn to know your sleep rituals.

In the book of Ecclesiastes we read of right times and right seasons. So I add this: "There is a time to sleep and a time to wake, a time for day and a time for night, a time for dark and a time for light, a time for talk and a time to be still." There is a time for sleep.

This is the time for sleep.

I KEEP LOOKING AT THE CLOCK.

If time ticks your waking hours away, stop the clock.

In my bedroom the face of the clock glows. For years it played games with me and won. It kept telling me what I did not really want to know: "What time is it now? How long did I just sleep? What time now? How much longer until I have to get up?"

In the dark I couldn't win against numbers glowing on a clock. I had grown too aware of half hours in the night. The clock was too bright and bold. It helped keep me awake.

I learned something that helped: I turned the clock around. I did not need a clock checking my sleep pattern. A stopwatch works well on a race track, but not in a bedroom.

Night is when angels keep watch over me. Night angels are in a prayer I have believed and prayed for seventy years. The glow of angels is more restful than the face of a clock. At night I look at angel glow.

Sometimes keep your clock out of sight. Think of night in ways other than hours of sleep. Spiritual powers keep watch through the night. Picture loved ones and angels and God offering love and rest. Image sleep as healing, recreation, renewal, refreshment. Prepare yourself for angel visits, angel glow at night. Get ready for sleep with a spirit of gratitude, forgiveness, kindness, love—a peaceful spirit.

In recent years I feel differently toward night clocks. Three striking clocks in my house keep time day and night. They are friends. I miss them when they are silent. They no longer break nighttime into pieces, into hours and half hours and minutes; they connect the night. When I hear a clock strike at night, I think of the ongoing gift of life.

Night hours are special. Sunset, darkness, midnight, striking clocks, starlight, moonlight, dawn—all have meaning for sleep. Time is a gift with moods, emotions, a spirit.

Be prepared to face a clock at any time—to see it, face it, or turn it to the wall, and to give thanks. There is a clock in you that knows when it is time to sleep.

I look at angel glow at night.

I WAKE UP TOO EARLY.

I woke when it was still dark. I looked at the clock; it was too early to get up. I wanted more sleep, needed more sleep. Daylight was barely beginning, and I was awake.

I looked out the north window. A surprise hurried across the patio. I had seen these creatures many times, but not like this, not during the period just before dawn. A raccoon, fur dark in the night, ran past my window. I watched the raccoon scurry up my elm tree. Up in a treetop a raccoon was glad for bird food it had scraped from the ground. Down here I was suddenly glad to be awake.

The raccoon and I had a meeting as dawn was breaking. Perched in our highest elm, the raccoon looked at me; I looked at the raccoon.

It was too early to be up; I knew I would miss the sleep later. But it was the right time for the raccoon and me to meet. I knew the raccoon would nap during the day. So might I.

For more than forty years, a good friend and noted scholar, Roland Bainton, napped midday. In hotel lobbies, in his car, at the library, I saw him napping. He had built midday rest into his daily calendar. "I never nap during the day if I want to sleep at night." I've heard that line; I've said it myself.

In my silent, early-morning conversation with the raccoon, I think I heard it say, "I nap in daylight. Try it."

It was too early to be awake. I hadn't wanted to be awake. But I'm glad I didn't miss that raccoon. The brief encounter was my morning star, my wake-up call. A raccoon and I met in the dark just before dawn. We studied each other. I felt blessed.

I will wake again before dawn. I will do so often. It is early spring, so much is beginning. Nature rises early. Robins are building nests. Three deer are crossing our yard. Where were they in the dark when the raccoon and I met? Maybe, on another early waking, I will meet a deer.

We do not always wake to see deer, robins, raccoons. But there are other surprises in the dark—trees, moon, sky, the night wind, falling stars, someone going to work, someone coming home. There is always something to see, to meet, to enjoy. I wake; it is there for me in the night.

Sometimes I read a psalm that begins, "The earth is the Lord's, and everything in it, the world, and all who live in it." I look out the window before dawn and see a star, a tree dancing in wind, a raccoon in an elm. It's true: "The earth is the Lord's, and everything in it."

We wake before we want to, it is still night. Sometimes we wake just in time to see what we'll always remember.

O God, show me a surprise at night.

My bed's uncomfortable.

Find pillows to cradle you.

A bed can feel too big when I toss and turn in the night. I roll around in too big a place. For good sleep I need to be held. I need boundaries. Sometimes I can't find my sleeping position for sleep. Should I face left or right, lie on my back or face down?

I am sure someone held me close when I slept as an infant. I think my mother cradled me in a way still known inside me.

I have pillows within reach to mark my sleeping place, to help me feel held. It began in a hospital after spine surgery. Pillows held me still so I did not hurt myself. Pillows hugged me when I leaned against them, kept me safe. I learned to like pillows, to use them. Now I sleep with four pillows at hand. I like feeling safe.

We all have comfort zones, different spaces we need for working, playing, loving, living, sleeping. We are territorial. We know the feelings of our possessions and places These are our comfort zones. I have learned to make my own sleeping zones—ways to sleep best, ways that wake me best. I know ways to lie for hours not moving and feeling fine.

Getting into a good sleeping position is like kneeling right for prayer, bending right to lift a heavy object, reaching right to a top shelf, showing reverence.

Decide how you relax best for sleep. Take care of little feelings your body has. Make sure your neck feels right, your head is turned so you breathe best. I like sleeping in three positions, and when I wake at night, I consciously move into the next position. I expect it to be right; I have done it for years.

I know children who travel with a pillow. It centers the space in which they sleep. After many years I find pillows give the soft feeling of a parent's lap to help me find my rest.

Someone is holding me; I am being held.

I NEED GOOD, NIGHT THOUGHTS.

I often have wakened at night hating the darkness. If only there were daylight.

One night I recalled good things that happened in the dark. "While it was still dark," the women ran to the tomb and found Jesus had risen. Easter came in the dark. I wonder how much of life is renewed in the night; how many get well in the dark; how many of us are reborn at night.

At night shepherds were startled by angels. Some left their flocks and ran to the Bethlehem inn. In the night, they beheld the mother with child, knelt, adored, and ran back to their flocks glorifying God. They could find their way for all this in the dark. There is sometimes a light we see only in the night.

"In the night in which he was betrayed," Jesus took the bread and the cup and hosted a holy meal. The sharing of that meal in the night has spread to all the earth. It was not just another dark night; it was "the night in which He was betrayed." Jesus took a long dark night and gave the world a holy supper. This meal has been a blessing for many people in their night.

No night is just another night in the dark.

In the dark, in the belly of a great fish, a prophet heard God's calling, went to preach God's truth and love in Nineveh, and saved a city. In the dark, Jonah knelt and heard about work to do. In the dark, when light is shut out, I can sometimes finally hear a message loud and clear: truth and love can dawn in the night.

In the dark, the Children of Israel started their journey to freedom. In the darkness of the Passover, they found their sign and strength. In a terrible night of the final plague, God started a nation walking to a promised land.

I sometimes sit at night in a favorite room with many windows. Some nights are very dark. I wait in the dark. Gradually the light of night grows. The sky gets brighter, shadows deepen; back lighting outlines nature. Tiny pieces of life unfold in the dark. There are shapes I never see in the day, moods that get lost in light. There are wonders to see in the night. There is a light we only know at night. We can learn to see in the dark.

O God, open my eyes in the dark.

RESTLESS, RACING THOUGHTS

God's peace is in me; God's peace holds me.

WORDS KEEP FLOATING THROUGH MY HEAD.

Find one word. If it fits, stay with it. Put it on.

Words get loose and fly in the night. Thoughts explode like popcorn and swirl in a whirlwind. Words flit through my head, feel heavy, bombard my mind. How can I control these forceful words of the night?

I lie awake and wonder. There are all these words in me. Each word is piece of my life, representing a person I know, leading to a familiar place, tracing back to a special time. We are all filled with the miracle of such night words. But too many words keep us from sleep.

When bombarded by words before sleep, I try to see them all as a word collage of myself. They represent my stories, my history, my fears, my hopes. They are my own catalogue, my life.

If I chase these words in the night, my mind spins, I stay awake, I worry. In this racing of thoughts, I borrow trouble, grow scattered, get unreal. I do not want night words to rob me of joy, trust, sleep.

They are my words, I can do what I want with them. I will choose just one good word, a word that fits the night. I will get close to it, ride it gently like the horse I rode as a child.

It is possible to choose one word to ride, a word that feels right. Keep the word calm, simple, still, loving. Wrap yourself in a word that comforts, like someone tucking you in at night. Rest in one good word, let it cover you like a blanket. Try to be inside the feeling of the word. It is possible to be cozy inside a warm word and sleep.

Sometimes the word is the name of a loving person, near or far. Stay with the name, stay with the person. The word may be a place or a promise. Stay in that place, stay with that promise to find sleep or rest. A good rest can be like sleep.

HERBERT BROKERING

These are rest and sleep words: "my shepherd; my cup runs over; forever; with you always; beloved."

These are words that comfort me, wrap around me, quiet me: "peace, mellow, rest, relax, yes, life, loved." If one of these fits you, put it on. Find your restful words.

If a thought comforts you, wrap yourself in it. If a word is calming, stay by it.

I have a peaceful word.

I'M ON A ROLLER COASTER.

I ride a roller coaster at 2 A.M. I wake, and I'm up or down, riding highs and lows. There is no even plain, no middle ground. Who can sleep riding a roller coaster?

In the night, when we wake on our ups-and-downs, we need to be known, felt, understood. We need something to fix our sights on, something that will ride with us. God knows. God's world is highs and lows.

I go to nature in my waking nights. Ocean waves mount high; they fall low. I ride the ocean at night; I soar high on waves; I go low. The ocean carries me. The ocean knows me. I know the ocean.

The sun knows my ups and downs: it sets, and it rises. During a long, sleepless recovery, I sat at a dark south window, waiting for morning. I watched sunlight pierce a dark horizon, burn through clouds with its early fire. I was down; the sun came up; I rode up with the power of the sun. I follow the path of the sun.

The seasons of the moon are medicine for my restless nights. The moon knows my spirit. I know the rising moon, the waning moon, the full moon. I sit by the window and watch the moon's highs and lows.

The night sky is full of kindred spirits. In the night I wake, and the stars wake with me. In the dark I look for falling stars, a rising moon, the glow of northern lights. At dawn I am friends with a rising sun.

My spirit knows cycles of seasons. Winter and summer are within me. My spirit, like seed, rests low under earth, breaks through, grows tall, blooms. The power of the seed rises out of the dark, from underground. My soul opens in the dark and rises to life.

Ecclesiastes lists the seasons of earth. The list of my life's seasons is long: a time for winter and for spring, a time for yes and no, a time for crying and cheering, a time for fear and trust, a time for hurt and healing, a time for running and patience—a time for all the ups and downs that are my life.

An oriole builds a nest, a wind blows the nest to the ground. Night passes. In the morning, the oriole sings and carries strings and sticks to weave a new nest. Life goes up and down. Life starts over and over. The oriole sings.

As it is in nature, so it is in human nature.

I cycle like the seasons. I am up; I am down. God is with me.

I WANT TO HOLD THAT THOUGHT.

I want to remember, so I write it down.

Sometimes I lie awake and my mind is full of things I want to do. The dark is a time for ideas. Ideas for a talk, a book, relationships, or work. Something I want to tell someone. A sentence or a word I want to keep in mind. These play tag in my mind.

At bedtime when my mind is full of things to do, I write them down on paper. There's a pad and pen on the nightstand by my bed. I may wake with new thoughts. I scribble them in the dark. If I'm alone, I switch on the light and sit up with thoughts and pen. Or I get out of bed to write. I make a list of things important at the moment, words or thoughts I don't want to lose. I do not study them, they are just notes for tomorrow.

The list may be short or very long. I enjoy the things I write; they are often what I look forward to, not things I dread. All these help empty my mind, like cleaning out pockets before putting clothes away.

The nightly list is also a profile of myself. On paper I see my values, hopes, ideas, worries, needs. It helps me peek into tomorrow, look forward, anticipate. I give myself an assignment, I get to choose it.

The other night I woke thinking of Evelyn Sakura, my new grandchild. What could I give her? A baby poem. Sakura means cherry blossom. I wrote "I'll meet you 'neath a cherry tree." I circled it and was ready for sleep. Here is one stanza I wrote in the morning:

> When I will find that cherry tree
> I know I'll find you there
> In purple robe and shoes of silk
> And blossoms in the air.

At night I saved a poem, a gift for my granddaughter. At night I have made inventories. At night I have begun stories and lyrics I love. My nighttime beginnings help me get a head start on the new day.

It's important to empty the mind, to let thoughts go, to pray, to meet night in a peaceful spirit. I write my thoughts, say my prayers, and wait for sleep, looking forward to the morning.

My thoughts are safe, I can sleep in peace.

QUESTIONS COME IN THE NIGHT.

My head is swimming with feelings, worries, ideas, dreams, expectations, persons. I don't know how to hold my mind still. If I could only sort through all my thoughts and feelings. If only I could find a way to calm my worries, my fears.

Asking good questions is half the answer. I have answers hiding inside me. I need the right questions to bring them out.

I know where to find good questions in a moonlit night. I look out the bedroom window. I see trees. I choose a blooming apple tree, buds bursting.

I am host. The tree is my guest. I ask the tree these five questions. How did you get here? Who thinks you're beautiful? Who cares for you in the dark? How do you rest? What do you do in a storm? The questions to the blooming apple tree quiet me. There is still in the night.

I choose one question and let it grow. I rest inside it. I make it my own. "Who thinks you're beautiful?" I know the answer in the night. Persons come to mind. I hear them, see them, feel them, love them. "Who thinks I am beautiful?" A right question for the night. Now I am more beautiful.

Thank you, blooming apple tree.

"What do you do in a storm?" I listen to the silence of the tree and hear the answers. I feel the tree lean on its roots, see the branches dance in wind, see its leaves wave in rain. That is the tree in a storm; what do I do in a storm? I see myself leaning, rooted, dancing, washed by rain. I remember running in rain. I remember watching a storm with Father, unafraid with him. I know the apple tree in a storm, I know myself in a storm.

I ask the tree, as I ask myself: "Who cares for you in the dark?" My thoughts stay with the apple tree. It is those who care in the light: the one who planted you here, children who lie in your shade, a woman who likes your blossoms, a neighbor who makes jelly, a man who likes apples. In the night, the children and the woman wake and remember the apple tree, the bloom, the shade, the jelly, the fragrance.

"Who cares for me in the dark?" There are those who remember us in the dark, who wake, then think of us, bless us, get excited for something we said or did, want to be with us, think we're beautiful.

A professor told me, "Ask a tree questions. They will be good questions for you to ask yourself." Ask a cloud, a river, a star, a shoe, a building, a book, a bird. Ask questions of someone close. Learn to ask good questions when you lie awake at night. Then listen for an answer.

A good question will help you find good answers in a sleepless night.

Good questions are good medicine.

I need something to do.

I woke and could not sleep. I needed something to do. No major project, something easy but important, something to make me feel worthwhile, alive.

I watered an African violet. I got out of bed and watered the violet. Then I sat beside it, waited there, rocking slowly beside a flower I had just given a drink. I watched the flower and was still.

The violet was not afraid of night. It met the night with petals open. Despite the night, it bloomed, even as it graced daytime. The violet was in good spirits.

I looked at the flower in full bloom. Purple pink is elegant against dark green. Beautiful. I felt more elegant, more beautiful. The violet silently showed me beauty, my beauty. We were side by side, face to face, together in the night.

The violet liked the drink, as do I in the night. A little water is good in a night journey when the body feels too warm, too alone. How often children wake in the night to say, "I want a drink." They want the water, and they want a friend. Water is more than water when someone gives us a drink on sleepless nights.

The violet and I were friends. Flowers are more than flowers when we care for them. They care for us, they bloom, struggle through neglect, hang on, reach deep into their roots, make it. We cheer them when they stay alive; they thank us if we listen.

Once this violet was weak, wilted, barely alive. Now I count seven blossoms. I count seven blessings in the night.

The outer leaves of the violet are brown, falling off. It is shedding what it does not need, cannot hold, what is over. The violet is letting go of what was once its new leaf. The violet and I will both let go of what is over.

The violet has tiny new leaves in its center. Violets grow from inside out. Its root is sending up new life. Like the violet, I am new from the center, from inside out.

The violet is not moving as far as I can see. I can almost hear the violet breathe, at peace with being a violet. I am finding my peace with being who I am. It is enough for me, now, to be myself.

I stayed by the violet for a while in the night; I found myself for a while. A little while is enough for now.

I am tending a flower; my life is God's flower.

I KEEP FORGETTING SOMETHING.

I am awakened in the night by something I want to remember: someone's name, a place, some event. What is it? Why can't I think of it?

I once remembered all such things, knew them by heart, recalled them at will. I knew hundreds of learning exercises—their purpose, their style, how they felt. And I knew poems, prayers, lyrics, names of people, inventories. My mind was full of them. Now so many are gone. In the dark waking of this night I am forgetful. And I am frustrated.

Then comes the thought, "I don't need it anymore. I can let these things go. Now I know new names, new places, new priorities. My mind is making room for something new."

A mind has its seasons, times come and go. A field changes flowers. Seed blows in, a new crop rises. So it is with the mind: new times, new priorities, new lists, new things to remember, new things to do. Life changes, the mind makes room.

I woke worried about forgetting, sorry for what I could not remember, frustrated. In a sleepless night I decide to let go of the forgotten thought, tell it good-bye. I will replace it with something else, a thought I need now—a good thought, a memory I've held onto, a new poem, a new song, a place I like, a person I love, a fresh idea.

There is too much to remember. We get to choose.

Years ago I woke in the night from pain that was always with me. Spinal surgery followed. People came to know me by my hurt. Years later, they still ask, "How's your back?" My back? Oh, my back! I had forgotten about that pain. Thousands of good times have replaced those hours of pain.

You have this waking time tonight, bothered by what you cannot remember. Forget what you forgot. Why worry about it?

Instead, fill the waking time with good new thoughts. There's always seed blowing in the wind, looking for a new place to grow. Seed plants itself, dies, changes, is new, transformed.

Worry hides wonder. I think of a seed. In a sleepless hour I trade my worry for God's wonder.

Practice forgetting. Let new memories grow.

O God, thank you for forgetfulness, thank you for memory.

I need soothing music.

There are lyrics in the Bible for sleeping.

"He makes me lie down in green pastures; he leads me beside still waters; he restores my soul." Lines from Bible songs quiet me in the night.

I believe in a higher power; I believe in God. I find songs for peace, rest, and comfort in Psalms. They contain quiet lyrics about God. They are good songs for the night.

Some songs I know by heart. I say them very slowly, each word washing over me. "The Lord is my shepherd . . . I shall not want. . . . He makes me lie down in green pastures . . . he leads me beside still waters . . . he restores my soul. . . ." This psalm has rested me a thousand times.

Other phrases of holy writings are also my friends in the night. But the psalms are my closest friends. I snuggle into their words, feel safe in their images. I trust their promises, while feeling their beauty. Psalms are a true and steady light in the dark.

Psalms put me touch with all people who pray in the night. They are proven prayers of grandparents, rabbis, priests, saints, kings, queens, evangelists, stars, heroes, children, skeptics, and believers. Psalms assure me that I am not alone. Their sacred words connect me with all those who have prayed through the ages, and to those who continue to pray. I feel their quiet power, their assurance, their invitation to rest. For me, psalms are a guarantee, offering proof, certainty, comfort.

Listen to the music of psalms during your sleepless nights. Turn to a favorite psalm; keep it near your bed. Read all of it or part of it. Find a word or phrase you like. Memorize a verse by heart. A word, a phrase, or a verse can cover worry like a quilt, like a comforter for the spirit. From the first twenty psalms, I have chosen five lyrics for sleepless nights:

[I am] like a tree planted by streams of water, which yields its fruit in season and whose leaf does not wither.
(Psalm 1:3)

When I consider your heavens, the work of your fingers, the moon and the stars, which you have set in place, what [am I] that you are mindful of [me] the son of man that you care for [me]? (Psalm 8:3,4)

I will praise you, O Lord with all my heart; I will tell of all your wonders. I will be glad and rejoice in you.
(Psalm 9:1,2)

I will praise the Lord, who counsels me; even at night my heart instructs me. I have set the Lord always before me. Because he is at my right hand, I will not be shaken.
(Psalm 16:7,8)

I love you, O Lord, my strength. The Lord is my rock, my fortress and my deliverer; my God is my rock, in whom I take refuge.
(Psalm 18:1,2)

Find your Psalm lyrics. There is music in the Bible to make night a friend.

I sing to the Lord: I am filled with soothing music.

My body won't relax.

To relax my body, I relax its many members, one at a time.

I hurt all over. It's hard to pinpoint what part of me keeps me awake. It could be an arm, or my legs, or my neck. Mostly it feels like my whole body.

How does one relax a whole body for rest, part by part, member by member? I begin with my feet and end with the top of my head. It is a ritual I know and follow by heart.

A relaxing exercise can be a spiritual journey, a prayer exercise. Talking to each member of my body, one by one, is like prayer traveling through the body. Each part of me hears the same good words. If I lose my thought, I return to the beginning of the exercise. It is the way I have prayed by heart from childhood. I pray my way through, to the end, with meaning.

I like prayer focused on my feet, then on my ankles, my knees, my hips, my spine—and all the rest. I pray over each part. A one- or two-word prayer connects me, makes me real, makes me whole.

My prayer is a single spiritual thought: "From God." "Yes." "Amen." "Relax." "Be well." "Thank you."

The body is gift from God. How restful to say "Thank you" to feet and hands and heart and lips; to say "Yes" or "Amen" to spine, eyes, forehead. "From God, from God, from God," lifts weight, vibrates, relaxes, gives peace to my ankles, hips, stomach, tongue, brain. It is like a gentle invisible massage.

In a college quartet I sang about how all body parts fit. "Dry Bones" is a prayer about a body connected by breath, by spirit, by prayer.

Sometimes I pray my body to sleep. The prayer travels. I feel weight in my feet lifted, flow through me, leave. I feel heartache give up its hold, disappear. I feel my eyes quit straining. They rest for not looking. I feel furrows in my forehead vanish.

When I find my prayer refrain, my focus, my blessing, I stay with it. I repeat it, a prayer by heart. I do not hurry the prayer. It is meant to lead me into sleep.

Sleep does not always follow, but I rest. An hour of sleep, an hour of relaxing prayer, may be the same.

God's peace is in me; God's peace holds me.

I worry and pray.

We were talking about sleep, about sleepless nights. I asked the young woman: "What do you do when you wake in the night?"

She answered quickly, "I pray. I pray." Then she added, "I worry a while, then I pray. First I worry."

She gathers her prayer list—the worries—then she prays. It's how she is.

I know this young woman well. She lights up when we talk about her mother. She is bonded to her mother, to her family, to home, to music, to holidays. She laughs easily, cries easily, worries easily, prays.

She works with handicapped children, knows each child by heart. She helps children sing without a worry; in song they look like they're marching into heaven. People applaud. She smiles. Parents think of her as healer. She reminds me of Jesus. Still, when she wakes in the night, she worries. Then she prays.

Worry, then pray. That's how many Psalms read. First the psalmist worries and complains, then he gives thanks and praise.

At night, I open up my worry box. Spread it out, all worries side by side. I sort through them, make worry clusters. Some are past, some will wait. Some are real, some hurt more. In the night, I choose my worries. Then I pray.

A window opens when I pray. The worries go up, out the window. Trust comes in. I give thanks. I grow calm. Most often then, I sleep.

"What do you do when you wake in the night?" The young woman was glad I asked.

I found an old song, Psalm 142: "I cry aloud to the Lord; I lift up my voice to the Lord for mercy. I pour out my complaint before him; before him I tell my trouble." That is how it begins. "Then the

righteous will gather about me because of your goodness to me."
That is how it ends. A prayer: we complain, we trust. Amen.

We who worry and pray in the night are not alone. We are
many. Worry, pray, then sleep.

Prayer is stronger than worry.

Fears in the Night

God's spirit is in me, is around me, is with me.

I'm losing my breath.

More than once I awoke at night with trouble breathing. I panicked. Something wasn't working. I began to hold breath in, to save it—a reserve, in case I might need it. Awake in the night, I was afraid of running out of breath.

I breathed shallow, rapidly, growing more and more frightened. I phoned my doctor for grounding. I heard a calm voice say, "Herbert, you're hyperventilating." I could feel compassion and understanding in his words.

"Breathe deeply," he said. Let it all out. Let it all out." I did, and my lungs kept filling with air—automatically. My breathing was better. The reserve I wanted was always there.

"It's working," I said. "My lungs keep filling with air." I was relieved, thankful. I can still hear my doctor's words, calming, soothing, "That's what lungs want to do, Herbert, fill up. Let it all out and fill up again."

In the night I learned of breathing medicine from my doctor. He drew pictures for his medicine. I can now visualize automatic reflexes. Breathing does not depend on me consciously inhaling and exhaling. Automatic reflexes are a miracle of the human body, of perfect design.

The psalmist sings, "Let everything that has breath praise the Lord." Breathing itself is a kind of praise. In the night, I picture the miracle of breathing as praising God. My fear of breathing is gone, the joy of breathing is back. Lions, kangaroos, snakes, doves, hamsters, poodles, elephants, alley cats, pigs, chickens, horses, cats, dogs, all breathe and praise God. "Let everything that has breath praise the Lord."

I remember our children as babies, their soft breath warm and even against my skin—a breathing miracle. When it's suddenly hard to breathe, picture breathing as an act of God, a miracle. Fill up, let it all out. Fill up, let it all out. Enjoy the breathing; give thanks for breath.

When I was little, we flew kites in the wind. I did not watch the wind, I watched the kite. The wind was always there, strong or gentle. Wind made the kite fly. Once the kite found the wind it leaned into the wind—loved, rode, climbed the wind.

For the kite and me, wind is there, breath is there. My kite did not fear the wind; it laughed in the sky. I am like the kite. I do not want the fear; I want the flight. I want to ride the miracle of breath, to laugh in flight.

A prayer of breathing begins: "Breathe on me, breath of God, fill me with life anew." Breath, wind, spirit, life—synonyms. Life is a gift, not to be feared but to be loved. Breathe deeply, take life, give praise. God is breath, spirit, holy spirit. We breathe, we inhale God's own spirit.

God keeps filling me with breath, with life.

I am breathing God's life, God's breath.

I don't know where I'm going.

How did I get to this point in my life? Where am I headed? What am I doing with my life? Is this a nightmare?

Problems loom bigger in the night. We feel keenly the loss of direction, aimlessness, uncertainty about life. When I wake in the night with these questions, I often think east, west, north, south. I'm a country boy, and directions are basic to me. I like to know where I'm going.

How often we're told we're "going somewhere": promoted up the ladder, to the top. Suddenly there are no more rungs; the top is a bottom.

We wake in the night and feel a sudden turn, a loss of direction, a dead end. Our horizons have disappeared, or we've lost interest in the direction we were headed. Or something happens and we can't get through a roadblock.

When I was little, our car sometimes got stuck in mud on a country road. Father would say earnestly, "We are stuck." I helped him jack up the car, clean mud off wheels and from under fenders, strap on chains, and push. Looking ahead did not get us anywhere. First we had to take care of the fact that we were stuck. First we had to get unstuck.

Being stuck can become a kind of rest stop along the way. It forces us to pause, to look around and assess. I can't go on this way. I need to look things over, to see which way I might proceed.

Sometimes a good question can help. What stopped me? Where am I? How did I get here? Who else is here with me? Where did I think I was going?

Where am I placing my energy now? What do I mean by "going somewhere?" Where do I want to be? How far is it? What are ways for me to go? How can I get help I need?

Sometimes my father and I walked home when our car got stuck. It was too dark to put on chains, so we waited until daylight. Sunlight helps us get unstuck.

I care about where I am going. I need to know where I am before I can go on.

O God, I see you are with me. I will follow you.

I'm scared.

Often I have wakened frightened. Was it a dream I had? Or is it real? In seconds, fear can change my heartbeat, my breathing, my vision, my balance. Fear has a power, a spirit of its own.

Why does fear increase inside us while we sleep? Why does it wait for the night to attack? Have you ever wakened and felt fear suddenly mount inside, fill you up? A bad scenario unfolds suddenly with one waking thought.

More than once when I have wakened in fear, I reach to someone nearby and say, "I'm scared." And the fear begins to leave me.

I name my fear aloud to God; it is no longer secret, it's in the open. And my fear begins to leave. I turn on a light; the darkness is broken. And my fear begins to leave.

I hear soothing voices: "You've felt this way before, and it turned out okay." "What did you do to get through this before?" "What do you think makes you feel scared?" "You'll be all right, just like all the other times." Someone used to say these things to me, and they eased my fear. Now I can hear them without waking anyone.

Fear does not like light. It does not want to be shared, to be shown for the coward it is. How quickly fear comes, how quickly it can go.

In the night fear comes to me like an old friend—not a dear friend, but someone I know well. I treat fear with respect. It can do me harm if I forget how to receive its visit.

A father took his own life. I went to the funeral, stood by his son. The young man looked frightened. I said to him, "If you ever need me, holler." I said it twice. "If you ever need me, holler." I wish I had said those words to his father.

If you're scared, holler for help. Someone who loves you will hear. Love is stronger than fear; love casts out fear.

O God, I'm hollering, you're hearing.

I FEEL LIKE I'M FALLING APART.

When I feel I'm falling apart, I stay with one of the parts to get a sense of being real.

Sometimes I lie awake and feel like there are too many parts. They move inside me like those little bumper cars at the circus, only now I'm not laughing. I'm between the cars, or I'm in all the cars. My insides tremble and shake. I feel like I may come apart.

Part of me is playing some tune I've had in my head since yesterday. Part of me carries on an old, heated conversation. Part of me is ticking off things I didn't get done for my trip. And part of me is saying, "I've got to sleep." These parts are all moving at once.

A friend of mine has a saying for times like this: "It's unreal." When I lie awake with these feelings, I say out loud, "I'm feeling unreal." Sometimes I say, "I don't like this. It really scares me."

To get real again, I touch something real: my hand (I think of all it has written, touched, held), a book by my bed (I think of what it's about), the colors in a Japanese painting (I met the artist in Tokyo). I stay with the thing. I pull myself together around it.

Or I say something coherent like, "I'm not alone. I've been through this before." Something that lets me hear myself being real, being together. Or sometimes I recall encouragement from my doctor, the exact words he said to me.

Sometimes I'll sit in an old green chair and say a Bible passage I remember: "I am with you always," or "With God all things are possible" or "The Lord is my shepherd." I say it out loud, and I say each word carefully, to give full attention to that word of God.

Then my insides start to come together around those words, that picture, that me who's real. When I'm whole again, I may sleep. I may get up and begin a new day. Or I may just stay still and give thanks.

My spirit is quiet. I am all together.

I'm up against a wall.

When I feel like I'm up against a wall, I lie awake staring at my wall, seeing nothing—nowhere to go, feeling stuck, feeling panicked. I'm up against a wall, so I'll see how I can use it.

I was twelve and dreamed to be a baseball star. I pitched a baseball against a bag of straw hanging on our tin barn. I felt confident that one day I would pitch like Lon Warneke of the St. Louis Cardinals, that one day I would hit home runs over the wall, out of the park.

In my first game, I broke my ankle. The doctor who examined me also heard a murmur in my heart. My baseball career was over at age twelve. I did not become a sports hero. I never hit a home run over a wall, as I had dreamed. I was up against a wall instead.

But I remembered that wall forty years later.

At that time, there were walls between nations—an Iron Curtain, the Berlin Wall. I looked at that wall: it was either a prison wall or a garden gate. I saw it as a gate, and took people through it for years. On the other side we found a beautiful garden. Going through that wall felt like hitting the home runs I had dreamed about.

Now that wall is down. There are always walls to break down, break through.

Sometimes walls are good. My feet swell easily, get heavy, become tired. If I come to a meeting late—standing room only—I look for a wall to lean against. A wall can be good.

Now when lying in bed, finding myself up against a wall and sleepless, I close my eyes and look carefully at the wall. If I need to, I can lean against it. If the wall is weak, perhaps I can get through. If it's wood, it may have a loose board. If it's not too high, I can look over. If it's got a window, I can look through and see what's on the other side. Maybe I don't even want to go there.

If the wall is strong, it might be a fortress to keep me from something harmful. I may see that God put the wall there to protect me. Maybe my wall wants to tell me something. It may be trying to slow me down so I can listen.

Swimmers know about walls. They push off with force from a wall that holds the water in. This may be a time for me to push off, to move in a new direction.

When I became a property owner for the first time, I cared a lot about my property line. I studied it; there were no plants or fences or walls to mark it. I had a line in mind. My neighbors also looked at that line from their side; they planted grass and lilacs on what was really six feet of my property.

Time passed, grass grew, lilacs bloomed. That line—that "wall"—is now a common garden. Our wall is filled with lilacs. I know now that a wall can bloom; it can bond people. In the night I look closely when I'm up against a wall. Perhaps my wall will turn into a row of flowers.

The wall feels good; I need a wall.

I can't see God.

Sometimes in the night I need a picture of God. It is not that I want to see God; I do not say "I can't see God." But I want to feel God. I want to be closer than from here to heaven. In the night I ask the question, "God, where are you?"

I was raised believing I could not see God. Not seeing God makes God bigger, more real, more grand, more powerful to me. God is spirit; imagining spirit is my most creative exercise. I imagine in a thousand ways; each image of God's spirit is at once new to me and old to me.

When little, in the night, I often woke screaming, frightened of a dream. Mother or Father came to hold me when I wakened. I was often cold, shaking, confused, frightened. The spirit of my mother and father holding me, was the spirit of God. They were my early imagination of God: personal, intimate, protecting.

Find an image of God that has a spirit of holiness. Stay with the picture, and let it be one image of God. Then find another image of holiness. Let that be another portrait of God. Picture God as spirit, holy. Keep these with you for nights when you ask, "God, where are you?"

The Bible gives us snapshots of God's spirit. Here are more images of God for a sleepless night; you can see them with your eyes shut in the dark:

God is like shade in the hot sun. God is like a rock in a flood. God is like a light on a hill. God is like free water for those who are thirsty. God is a shepherd hunting a lost lamb. God is like a father receiving a lost son. God is like a woman finding a lost coin. God is like the owner of a vineyard. God is like a soft wind before a cave.

In a sleepless night God is not my theologian. God is my nurse, my doctor, my mother and father, my good friend, my counselor, my soul mate. My imagination can not make God too small or too large or too near. God's spirit is smaller and greater and closer than I know. In a sleepless night, picture God as near, kind, safe, forgiving, watchful, loving, awake.

Spirit space is reality we do not see. I walked through an ancient historic site with students. One student placed his hands on walls and doorways that had been touched by ages and ages of hands. He walked on steps worn by feet no longer visible. He felt the past, felt the lives. He was in touch with reality in spirit.

In a sleepless time, touch reality in spirit.

God's Spirit is in me, is around me, is with me.

I'm slipping away.

I felt I was coming apart, a wobbling piece of clay on a spinning wheel, out of kilter, off center.

I sat up to give my thoughts a balance. The coming apart began in my mind, ran through my body. I could feel parts of myself; they wobbled, shook, felt separated. My breathing was irregular, shallow. What if I ran out of breath?

My concern went toward my feet, to my back, into my eyes, my lungs, my heartbeat. Each part of me seemed troubled. I wobbled on the wheel, ready to fly apart.

"Center the clay, center the clay." My son is a potter. I've seen him work, watched him center clay on his wheel. I knew what the words meant. Be centered.

Adam means red clay. The first man was formed from clay. All humans are clay, turning, being shaped. I was turning, but I wobbled on the wheel in the night.

Be centered. Breathe. Breathing is how we center. What centered me most quickly was regular breathing: inhaling, holding, counting, exhaling, holding, counting. I breathed deeply, exhaled deeply. Breathing gave my body balance.

I set my breathing to a tempo, sometimes holding a deep breath and counting three, exhaling and counting three. Sometimes I counted four or five, sometimes longer for inhaling than exhaling.

Breathing came natural, restful, in rhythm. It came as dance. I forgot about the breathing; I enjoyed the breath. Centered breathing improves the spirit.

In a wobbling night, center your breathing. Center your spirit. Breath means spirit, life. I told this to friends. They added visual pictures of breathing.

One is a fisherman. He pictured reeling in the parts that scatter, wobble, are out of control. He reeled in each wobbly part until he was breathing safely in a fishing boat.

Another pictured a homemade cake falling apart, in pieces. It was all crumbling on a platter. While breathing in rhythm, she frosted the cake, pouring chocolate into the cracks and crevices. The cake was whole; she put it together with frosting. It was delicious—better than before. She breathed more easily serving a delicious homemade cake.

Find your picture for breathing, centering. Regular breathing itself is a restful image. Breathe, breathe, breathe. The fun of breathing—centered, in rhythm—is a like a dance we know by heart. Find your breath, find your image. In the night, when your body wobbles, center your spirit, your breath.

God is breathing in me; I breathe God's spirit.

RESENTMENT AND ANGER

I am forgiven. I forgive.

IT'S ALL RIGHT TO KICK AND SCREAM.

But then make up.

"No, No, No!" I kicked and screamed as child. When I hurt, I hurt. When I was angry, I was angry. And when I loved, I loved.

Sometimes I still need to kick and scream. I can't get to sleep at night until I do. I kick and scream aloud. I do it quietly. Mostly I do it without a sound. I have to feel my problem, feel my anger. Until I kick and scream, I cannot feel relief, resolution. I cannot get to sleep.

I have downs and ups. I doubt and I trust. I have anger and tears, joy and peace. I am all these things. What do I do with tears, anger, pain? I recognize them as real. I look for a cause, see what sparked the feeling. I show my hurts. It is okay for me to kick and scream.

I have found ways to work through hurt, disappointment, anger, toward a happy resolution.

Here is a scenario: Something happens and I feel put down. I may speak out, feel resentment, or scheme to retaliate. I lie awake thinking about what I did, what I didn't do, what I wanted to do. Then I kick and scream—get all the feelings out. I kick and scream to God. No lies, no blaming, no justifying; only feelings—scream until I'm empty. I can feel God sigh, smile, love me. Then I think of how to redeem things, to make up. I resolve to do good. I feel better than ever.

"I hate you." Then, "I love you."

My kicking is not meant to hurt, it is my complaint. Kicking breaks open my evil spirit, makes me honest, shows my soul. Lets me heal.

Sometimes my gripe, my complaint, my kick, is against God. I have learned to scream, shout, complain to, kick against, my highest power. I do not hold back my hurt, anger, mourning. I will not hide these feelings from God. The psalms show me how:

For I eat ashes as my food and mingle my
drink with tears because of your great
wrath, for you have taken me up and
thrown me aside. My days are like evening
shadow; I whither away like grass.
(Psalm 102:9-11)

And the psalms show me how to move from kicking and screaming to praise and love:

But you, O Lord, sit enthroned forever;
your renown endures to all generations.
You will arise and have compassion on
Zion. (Psalm 102:12-13a)

I was raised not to let the sun go down upon my wrath. Before I can sleep, I must kick and scream my wrath, my hurt, my sorrow—and move past them into peace, joy. If the sun sets on my wrath, I wake in the night.

O God, I kick and scream, and I love you.

I'm not appreciated.

If people don't appreciate who I am, I'll wrap myself up as a gift to give them.

I don't sleep well when I feel unappreciated. What do I do? As I lie awake I plan: I'll quit, retaliate, get even, withdraw, tell someone off. All these are possible solutions. All these are also stressful. They make me feel tired—but not in a way that helps me sleep. Self-pity and retaliation are illnesses that rob us of valuable sleep.

I want to be taken as special, not taken for granted. I want my life to be an instrument of peace, hope, fun, love, beauty. I want to belong, to be someone who is wanted and needed. What can I do to be appreciated?

I will close my eyes and see myself as a gift. I will gift-wrap myself, think of ways to give away who I am and what I do without strings attached. I will loosen each string I tie to the things I do for others, to the gift of myself. I will ask God to create in me a new and clean spirit so my gift is whole, good, free.

Then I will think of those who do not appreciate me, those who have not welcomed me, those who bother me, whose feelings wake me in the night. I will look at them now not as enemies but as friends, perhaps sisters or brothers, who need what I am and do. I will picture them enjoying my presence, thanking me for what I give, smiling, looking at me in love.

As I picture others accepting me, I will look again at how I present my work and self to them. I will imagine what I give them as enriching their lives.

Once I brought a pumpkin to a graduate class I was teaching. A new student objected to this silly waste of time. He was angry with me. He had not yet given himself fully to the community of students. During break time I gift-wrapped the pumpkin and gave it to him. For the next week he struggled with my gift and with our relationship. One day he brought the pumpkin to class, carved and with a candle inside. We exchanged the same gift. We learned how we are gifts to each other.

"I don't feel appreciated. I didn't like a cutting remark. Why don't I feel included?" More than once, in the night, my prayers about these things have turned into poems. Hymns and lyrics for anthems, gifts to those from whom I have felt cut off. Through songs I have given myself as gift.

I like seeing myself and others as gift-wrapped. We are gifts from God.

"You are a gift. Thank you for your self." There was a time I answered, "It's nothing." Now I say, "You're welcome."

I am someone's gift. I am giving myself away.

People owe me.

I have kept borrowed items far too long: a rake, shovel, hammer, pipe wrench, umbrella, pen, binoculars, chair. Every time I saw the thing I felt bad, guilty. Until these were back with their owners, the debt was on my mind.

Itemizing my debts—writing down a list—is good. It helps me remember.

Itemizing debts others owe us—keeping a list of grievances and resentments—is bad. It won't let me forget.

I recall the country store of my childhood. Our grocer wrote his debit column in red. Credits were blue or black. If the red column got too long, the grocer was in trouble.

A long red column (a list of things owed to us) can mean trouble. It can rob us of sleep. In graduate school, I learned that blue walls are soothing, pink walls arouse emotions. It is hard to sleep when there's a red column in our minds.

I can't sleep when a list of others' debts feels big around me. I toss and turn when filled with grievances against others, anxiety and resentment others caused me, anger over wrongs others committed. My debit list robs me of peace, of rest.

Freedom from debt frees both the debtor and the one owed. Love cancels debts; love forgives, frees. When I am free, I can sleep.

How do we cancel debts in the night? Write a note of forgiveness. Make a phone call. Whisper a good word to someone so you hear it yourself. Bless from a distance. Plan to make amends. If someone nearby owes you, wake the person and cancel the debt. Forgiveness will give you both a better sleep.

We are created for kindness, not hurt; for love, not resentment; for forgiveness, not debt. In the night, love can move us from the red into the blue. We sleep best in a blue room.

I am forgiven. I forgive.

MY FRIEND IS BECOMING MY ENEMY.

Nighttime is for building up friends. We make plans together. I can hardly wait. I am counting on what we decided. Then something happens, plans change. I feel let down.

I do not know the reason for the change of plans, only that they change. In the night I pretend to know. I begin guessing. The list grows long. My spirit grows dark in the night. I feel taken for granted; I imagine things about my friend, about myself. Am I losing my friend? I put the worst construction on a single change of plans.

In the middle of the night I feel disappointment, resentment, anger toward a friend.

In the night I am wide awake. A tiny change of plans has grown into a grandiose worry. I am doubting a good friend. I whisper my anger, my resentment. I think of things to say, to write, to do, to get even. I am angry against my friend and I cannot sleep.

Then I pray for other thoughts, for memories. I think of old times, good times, good feelings, a good friend. In the night I begin to make up with my friend. I think on our friendship, on a person I have long trusted. I remember laughter, the good times. I smile in the night. I know there is a good reason for the change of plans. I will ask; I will trust the friendship.

In the night a friendship can grow. I will think good about the person, feel good feelings, have good thoughts. Good feelings and thoughts soon turn to blessing, calm, prayer. In the night watch I thank God for my friend.

In a sleepless night, friendships can be broken or built up. Pray for pictures of good times, value friendship, hear laughter, remember kindness, think of gifts exchanged, build trust, be forgiving.

Night is a good time to build up a friend, to value a special treasure.

I am making a friend in the dark.

IMAGES CAN HURT; IMAGES CAN HEAL.

Images can be medicine for sleep.

There is not much I cannot imagine. What I visualize can become real to me. Visualization is stronger than pretending. I can imagine hurt, pain, sorrow. In the night, I sometimes see pictures that rob my rest. In the night I also can find healing images, images that bring rest.

We all imagine, visualize, picture. These are gifts we have from birth. We develop meaning through picturing. These inner images are visual, sensual, emotional, physical, spiritual.

Imaging can make us sick. My father felt symptoms of patients he visited. I can picture pain and disease so vividly that they hold me. As a child, I pictured myself having polio, diphtheria, even a goiter. I pictured myself in an iron lung like Raymond, down the country road. I imagined myself with a heart problem like Walter in a nearby town. I thought I was growing a goiter like Mrs. Henry. These images did not help me sleep or make me well.

Pictures of fear and anger also keep me awake.

Forty years ago, a colleague helped me see how writing is healing. I imagined and wrote poems and stories using pictures, images, emotional sketches. I wrote and said what I saw in good images. Visualizing became restful for me. I turned daily problems into gentle parables. Many were published. The writing healed me, the reading healed others.

There are places to imagine and many scenes to sketch that can calm a spirit. Good images are near. Find a healing image and stay with the picture into sleep.

We all know paintings by heart. I like the ones in my bedroom: the beauty and soft swaying of a field of bluebonnets; the shimmering water of Lake Chelan; a refuge with family and friends in the Cascades; a painting by Watanabe of Japan and the cherry blossoms I pretend to see in it. *I* choose. I can sleep by bluebonnets, by water, by cherry blossoms.

In my dresser is a watch I inherited. In the night, I find rest seeing that watch in the hand of my mother, her gift to my father eighty years ago. The image of my mother's kind spirit is restful to me.

Imagine gentle spirits in the night and feel their calm. Find peace beside some water, beneath cherry blossoms, in a meadow of blue bonnets. Any place or time has images for sleep. I can make the choice.

I can sleep inside a good picture.

FEELING LOW IN THE NIGHT

Someone is praying for me right now.

I can't find a rainbow.

I'm caught in a flood. The sky is dark, threatening; the water is rising all around. Help! God, please find me an ark. Or send a rainbow. It's dark and frightening in here.

There have been nights I awakened in storms of darkness and depression. I was caught in flood waters, and I was sinking. I needed a rainbow, some sign of hope.

For many years I led pilgrimages to what was called an iron-curtain country. In rooms far from home, I woke in the night and felt darkness, fear, loneliness. I remembered the rainbow after the Flood. I wanted a rainbow for myself those nights, but I couldn't find one. Where was the rainbow? I drew one over myself, sketched one in the air as if I were a child.

I met a rainbow minister in that cloudy Iron Curtain country. He and his parish often hosted us pilgrims. He knew the dark. And he knew about rainbows, about promise and hope. He greeted us with ringing bells and songs. Karl Heinz was our rainbow in dark nights in a dangerous, dreary time.

We said good-bye and went home again.

It was a dark Saturday night in Minnesota. It was a dark night for me, too. In a few hours, Karl would preach at his church thousands of miles away. In my night I phoned him in his morning.

"What will you preach tomorrow?" I asked. Long distance, he told me about the rainbow and the Flood. I listened; I was Noah in my dark flood. He told me how the rainbow did not appear in bright skies; it appeared in dark clouds. That is what I needed to know. Rainbows appear in cloudy skies.

Years later, someone brought me a rainbow cloth from Guatemala. I needed a rainbow. I have one from Guatemala. I hollered, immersed in my flood, and God heard me.

Sometimes in the night I need a rainbow. Though the sun is not risen, I see rainbows in the dark—hand woven in Guatemala, preached in an Iron Curtain country, scribbled in the air above me. There are rainbows for us in the night.

The great reformer, Martin Luther, knew storms and floods. And for many years, he could not find God's rainbow. Danger beat against his ark. He felt God's wrath, his own remorse and guilt. In the darkness of a castle, Luther was afraid during sleepless nights. Once more he read in Scripture what he had often read. This time, while in a stormy cloud, Martin Luther found God's rainbow. He believed God's rainbow promise: "I will not destroy you."

One stormy day in Erfurt, Germany, where Luther studied, I saw a double rainbow. Erfurt is near the home of the rainbow minister who told me long distance in the night, "Rainbows appear in clouds."

I wake in the night and look for a rainbow. If you can't find a rainbow, draw one over your head by heart. Remember a real rainbow from your childhood. Remember the end of the flood. Remember God's promise.

I see a rainbow over my bed.

I GIVE UP.

I give up. Three words that keep me from sleep, sink my spirit with their admission of failure. I can't do it. I lose. I'm a loser.

Where does this feeling come from? Is this the end of a dream? Of a rope? Of a career? Is this the end of a relationship? Did I lose? Was I bought out? Was I taken over? Am I surrendering? Why am I thinking the words "I give up"?

In a sleepless night, stay with the words. Play with their meaning. Be creative, not defeated! Ask questions such as: What will I give? Is giving up the end? Or does giving up mean someone gets to have what I have? Can giving up mean sharing with another?

"I give up" can be like a relay race, a turning something over to another. Now someone else gets to do it. How can I pass on what I have to the next runner? How can I surrender *and* win?

Is this something I need to let go? Can I give it up to God—and really let it go?

"I give up" may be the end of a road, but it isn't a dead end. Maybe it's time for a turn, a new direction. A new possibility.

I see a shepherd in England in the dark, uprooting a sapling he has watched grow. The root is bent, the stem is strong. The small tree surrenders, is uprooted, gives itself up. The shepherd turns the tree over; the tree is now a shepherd's staff. The root is now the crook of the staff.

"I give up" can mean more than "I quit." It can mean, "I am turned over, not destroyed; I am transformed, changed into something new." Relay race. Cleansing. Bend in a road. Shepherd's staff. Transformation.

A blessing in disguise.

O God, you take it from here.

I NEED A HUG.

Have you ever wakened and wished for a hug? Sometimes we just need to be held, especially in the dark hours of night. Plan to get your hug. Hugs are important; people need hugs.

In graduate school I studied babies with low intelligence quotients. In a research program these babies were held and rocked. Their IQs rose. The babies grew in mind and spirit.

I like to hug. My parents did not hug each other in front of the children. I did not see farmers hug when I was little. I saw farmers cry, laugh, shake hands, but never hug. I saw their wives hug. They hugged at funerals, at weddings, and when babies were born. They hugged children. They hugged each other.

We have always had kittens and cats in our family. They were always hugged, they always hugged back. One cat did not return our love. It came to us late in its life; it came to us scared—a fraidy cat. It was afraid to be held, afraid to be hugged. It slept afraid. It died afraid and alone.

A hug is not hard to have. It belongs to a family, to friends, to colleagues, to neighbors. If you really need a hug in the night, wake someone nearby and say, "I need a hug." See what happens. It will be worth the wake.

The one you want to hug may not be near. Hug them in your mind, in prayer, in your feelings. Stay with them in your spirit. Or get out of bed and hug them by phone, by letter, by E-mail. We can give and take hugs in many ways.

Do you need a hug in the night to help you sleep? Get a hug. If you can't hug in person, close your eyes and hug long distance. It was by being held and hugged that we first learned to sleep.

O God, give me a big hug.

It's taking so long to get well.

Night after night I lie awake. I am recovering.

In the dark I think of my slow, slow progress. Nights are longer. They stretch out, slow down, last and last. Sleep doesn't come.

My mind stumbles onto a healing thought: recovery rhymes with discovery. Recovery—discovery. These have to do with each other.

I have a new idea. I will use these sleepless times for discovery. What am I learning about myself, about someone else, a relationship, my spirit?

I take ten minutes and discover a miracle I overlooked in my recovery: a wound that healed, breathing that deepened, a bone mended. Recovery has to do with breath, blood, nerves, tissues, muscles, cells, emotions. I will think about the miracle of recovery.

Weeks go by, then months. There's this new kind of time— waiting. Time to discover meanings: the meaning of friends, family, recollections, making plans. A time to connect with someone I neglected, someone I rejected, a person lost in a busy shuffle, someone else who is waiting. Recovery gives me time.

I was told recovery would be slow, fast, average. I heard all these. Recovery takes time; but it can be special time. A chance to discover priorities, wants, gifts, emotions. What do I value most? What do I miss doing? Who are my dearest friends? How do I show gratitude? How patient am I?

I have time to meet myself again during my waking nights.

Della Mae is recovering. It is a miracle, the doctors say. The greater miracle is the discovery she has made. She wakes early. "I'm here for a purpose," she tells me. "I pray for others. They know I pray well. I am busy praying now." Della Mae is ninety-four. She is discovering prayer.

I wake and discover new time, time to feel thanks, to give thanks. How grateful am I for favors, sacrifices, kindness, gifts? Gratitude needs time. How kind am I? I have time to grow my good spirit.

In the night I have five minutes I could not find in the light. I have time to reconnect with persons I love, need, admire, honor. I have time to discover memories I cherish, time to review good life past, good time for today.

A composer sent me tunes he had written during his long recovery. I wrote lyrics for the tunes. I was in long recovery. We have twenty songs born during recovery. Time for twenty new songs.

God appeared to believers in a cloud, in the night, in a midnight voice, in waking visions, in silence. The word of God comes in the quiet dark. When time is long, I can listen for God.

Recovery time is fuller time. A pendulum swings wider. Clocks tick louder, strike longer. Value increases. Recovery time is healing time, discovery time, holy time.

O God, I am growing new, I am always healing.

I'm afraid it's over.

Something important is over.

I failed at work. I lost a friend, a loved one. I ruined a relationship. I lie awake, knowing it is over. And there's nothing I can do. A feeling of something good destroyed is in me, and feelings of failure, loss.

I watched hail come to Nebraska fields when I was a boy. In two minutes, a harvest was beaten into the ground. Stalks were stripped, beards of barley broken. It was over. As a boy, I knew it was over.

I remember the farmers. I watched Mr. Geyer and Mr. Sodman after storms. They sang as loud as ever in country worship, and then stood around in the parking lot smiling, sharing hope, telling jokes as before. On Monday, they plowed and harrowed, worked on machinery, did chores, and sowed winter wheat. On their faces I saw it was not over.

What is my medicine in nights of failure and loss? The faces and faith of farmers. In the night I see the faces of Mr. Geyer, Mr. Sodman, Mr. Hertlein, Mr. Haecker, Mr. Hofling, Mr. Bauman, Mr. Doetker, Mr. Cramer. In the dark, I watch Mr. Spilker resow fields of corn after a hard rain.

At midnight, 1 A.M., or 4 A.M.—any time when work seems ruined, a relationship has died, a loved one has left, when I have failed—I find hope in faces of farmers I knew sixty years ago. I can still see these faces when I wake in the night.

"It's over." Our family felt this. At age eighteen, my brother fell from a willow tree and died. I was only nine. I woke feeling how much was done, over, finished, quit, dead. Many know this feeling. It woke me many nights.

On Sundays I watched the farmers' faces, listened to songs they sang, the words they said, the prayers they believed. Their faces proved again, it was not over. With them I learned to believe in planting winter wheat, and to hope for the green springtime.

I once kept an apple, saved it for years. It passed through seasons. Very slowly it turned to ashes. Ashes. Ashes. Spring. Spring. The ashes are earth, food for an African Violet. It is not over. Ashes, then Spring.

When you wake at night and it feels like it's over, remember faces. Look at faces in the dark—faces who knew to look beyond endings, to expect new beginnings. Remember those faces? Wait. Hope. It will grow.

What seems ended will grow again. Nothing is ever over.

I'M AT THE END OF MY ROPE.

If I'm at the end of my rope, I tie a knot, hang on, and swing for fun.

It's hard to hang on to a rope in the light, harder to do it in the dark. If it's too scary I close my eyes.

I've heard lots of advice about what to do when at the end of your rope. It doesn't always work. Years ago I heard I had cancer. I had a lot of sleepless nights then. A lot of time at the end of my rope.

My clearest picture of the end of a rope is our children hanging on tight to a knot, swinging out over a valley, feeling the excitement of risk and danger. Fear and fun are often near each other. Sometimes children want me to ride "Into the Future" at the Mall of America. In a dark room, sitting strapped secure, riding at high speed through caverns and between skyscrapers, I hang onto my seat. It's like hanging on to the end of a rope. I hang on tight, scream for fear and fun. Tears of fright and delight run over my face. For a long five minutes I join children at the end of some rope, hanging on, looking down, sometimes closing our eyes, screaming.

When I heard I had cancer I lay awake hanging onto the end of my rope. It was a new rope, a new fact. One night I tied a knot in my rope and swung out. Here was a new valley over which to swing. Lots of danger and risk. Lots of new possibilities. I said a prayer and closed my eyes and swung and looked below. I felt fun and fear. Trust holds the knot at the end.

Sleep didn't always come. But I wasn't just hanging, I was swinging on my rope, looking at possibilities.

I keep moving out and over new things as I swing on my ropes. I swing with others who are on the edge of the same valley. It is surprising how many have the fears and hopes and dreams I have.

Many have the same disease and wants, the same needs. We swing together. We learn to tie new knots, hold on, and swing again.

I know others are watching the way I swing for fear and for fun, holding on and swinging. We all watch each other at the end of some rope. God watches and holds tight. That's the grip that holds me.

God is holding my rope. It will let me swing.

I'm feeling down.

When I'm down, I touch the earth.

I wake up; I feel down. I could have written the song, "Sometimes I'm up, sometimes I'm down, O yes, Lord." All of us are down sometimes. Some of us sleep a lot when we're down—too much sleep. Not I. More often I lie awake, wanting sleep to return.

When I'm down, I look at the earth. Forty years ago I felt down, low, low to the ground. My doctor gave me good advice: "Touch earth every day."

God's earth is kind, healing, tender. Think of medicines Mother Earth grows and gives through plants and minerals. Think of the healing power in the ground. No wonder my doctor said, "Touch earth every day."

Some people touch earth in gardens; digging, planting, transplanting, and weeding are their medicines. Whenever I press my fingers against earth, hold a dusty stone on purpose, feel an autumn leaf crumble in my fingers, rub bark, I feel better. Often, when leading a group in some new retreat, I crush leaves or hold a dusty stone to begin. I make friends with this new place. Then I feel grounded.

When I can't sleep because I'm feeling down, I go down—to the earth. Down is not a bad direction. I watch October leaves tumble, watch seeds falling to the earth, see roots sending their tendrils down, touch snowflakes and raindrops on their way down. Down is a good direction.

Thoughts sink in, gravity holds us safe to earth, the sun sinks into the horizon. I ride down with these as I lie in bed. I enjoy the ride.

When we were little, we lived down low, close to Mother Earth. We played on the ground. We delighted in grains of sand, blades of grass, piles of twigs, cracks in the earth, dewdrops up close.

Herbert Brokering

Sometimes I get out of bed and become like a child. I go outside in the light of the moon and touch earth. I look at earth up close. I press into the soil and rub it between fingers. I pick a blade of grass, chew it, blow it like a whistle, smell its earthiness. I lean against a tree and say thanks.

When I'm down, I look down and around and underneath. Then I look up.

I am grounded. Earth heals.

I NEED TO FEEL LOVED.

I wake needing to feel I am loved. What happened in my life that makes me need to hear this over and over? "You are loved." In a single mailing I can receive letters of thanks, projects on which to collaborate with composers, assignments to lead retreats, accolades for lyrics I have written. And yet, in the nighttime I wake wondering about my worth, my value, my being loved.

Where do I go on such nights? To what is unseen, but real. I go to words I have heard, times I remember, persons who are fast sleep who love me, to promises of God. Invisible, yet I can see them in the dark.

I believe in the unseen. I look into the unseen. I learn in the dark.

"Prove it." The disciple Thomas said he could not believe in the Resurrection unless he could put his fingers into the wounds of the risen Jesus. He saw, he touched, he believed. Jesus told him, "Blessed are those who have not seen, and yet have come to believe." Awake in the night, I do not see, and I believe.

Most of what I believe is invisible. It is out of sight, in the past, coming tomorrow, distant, inside me, between two people, inside someone I love. This was more than a dawning, it was revelation, a surprise. I count on what I cannot see. I am committed to what I cannot touch. I believe in what first appears to have no substance, that which is invisible.

In the night, the invisible looms great. Spirit likes night. Love loves night. In the dark of a sleepless night, look for what is invisible, powerful, loving, joyful, sure. It is possible to find stability in the night.

I watched a child wait in an airport. The excitement on her face was from the mind's image of her father coming home, the feel of his arms around her—even though he was still in flight. The child looked forward to, anticipated, being with her father who was still in row 37-D on a 747. The child radiated hope.

"I believe." There is a way to see what isn't here, what you can't touch now, what will be, what was. In the dark I feel love, hear the words "you are loved," enjoy this power of the unseen.

I have practiced being loved—believing in love—mostly in the night.

Believing is being loved. God believes in me; God loves me.

I WAKE WITH A SINKING FEELING.

I wake with a sinking feeling. Everything is heavy: my thoughts, my feelings, my heart. My body feels heavy. I am too heavy to walk, too heavy to fly, to talk, to dream. I need a place that will hold my heaviness.

The Lord is my rock. I remember a line from an old, old song. "The Lord is my rock, my fortress, and my deliverer, my God, my rock in whom I take refuge." I find this line stronger, greater, heavier than my spirit. I rest on that rock.

Here are some thoughts to settle me down on the rock, to settle my dark heaviness. They may be your thoughts on a sleepless night.

I am on a rock, a great rock, a rock bedded deep in the earth. This is a rock I can climb, a wide rock, so I will not fall off the edge. It is a flat rock, on which I can lie; a jagged rock, into which I can crawl, against which I can sit and lean. This is a cool rock in summer, a warm rock in winter. This is a rock on which to rest. I am on a great rock.

"Rock of ages, cleft for me, let me hide myself in Thee." I remember another old song.

I am on a rock that was here long, long before me. Others have rested here; I am not the first. The rock is here for me, it is here for others; it will always be here for anyone. I am alone on the great rock, but there is room for another, if I want—room for many others. It is a resting place, I am on bedrock. I am on the foundation of my life, of all life. This is the rock where the earth is safe, where life begins, where I begin. I am resting where I will always be, on a rock.

The rock is the rock of God, the rock from creation. I am part of creation. It is the seventh day of creation, the Sabbath of God. I am resting in the day of rest, on the rock of rest and peace. I am being held by God the rock.

It is like lines from another another song I know: "On Christ the solid rock I stand, All other ground is sinking sand." I feel strength beneath me, I will not fall. God the rock is my strength. I am safe, secure.

I feel light. The rock is heavy. I am light, my thoughts are light, my feelings are light. I am light as a feather, on a rock. I can sleep in peace.

I stand on a rock. God is my rock.

Who can I touch in the night?

Touch a pet.

If you need a touch in the night but don't want to wake someone, wake your cat, dog, bird.

I have wakened suddenly feeling out of touch, feeling the need to be in touch, the need to touch. But it's night time, and everyone is asleep. There's a time to touch and be touched, to cuddle and be cuddled, to hold and be held. And there is a time to wake and to sleep. This is a time to sleep. Whom do I touch?

I know someone who in sleepless nights holds her cat. She pets, strokes, cuddles her cat in the dark. She feels her kindest feelings, speaks her kindest words, shares dreams, shows her best side to her cat. Touching a cat often helps her find her feelings, stay in touch in a sleepless night. She believes God is present in these moments, too.

A cat or dog likes being wakened for holding, touching, feeling loved. A pet will love and lick and purr, night or day, in sickness, in health, for better, for worse. A pet can sense my heart, feel my fear, and show affection in the night. A pet wants to be a friend.

Stroking, petting, holding a pet close can build up my feelings bank account. Feelings live deep inside; touches stay with us. All my childhood touching is stored inside me. I have memorized feelings sixty years old, put there by little white terriers. When I was little I got these feelings from my dog.

If you have a pet at hand on a sleepless night, touch it gently, say good words, watch it breathe, look into its eyes, feel its warmth, smile, ask it questions, watch closely for an answer, feel its life. Animals can read the heart.

A friend told me of the death of her cat. One son drove four hundred miles to be with Tai, their cat, in its final hours. He and his brother, now men, took turns cuddling Tai through night, until its death. They had cuddled the cat since they were children. Their hurting hearts could be eased only by holding Tai close, through the darkness. The brothers filled their feelings bank for ten hours, touching, holding, being loved, by Tai the cat.

I still draw on good childhood feelings from touching the animals in my care. I am often grateful for how they let me reach to touch them when I need holding.

Animals are family, especially in the night. Touching a pet in a sleepless night is a creative act. Animals love to be loved, loved to be touched. So do we.

O God, touching brings me peace. Thank you for pets.

Prayer multiplies in the dark.

"Hear my prayer, O Lord."

Walter was active for his age. He catalogued his large stationery store, knew all the items, each had a number. This was before computers. Walter knew every piece of merchandise by heart. He gave work everything he had. His heart was in his work.

Then Walter was sent to bed. It was a new time for him. He stayed quiet, lay long hours, waking and sleeping. Day and night blended.

He would not count inventory for a while. He would not help the store restock. He would not meet sales people who came and went, some for forty years. Walter was learning to lie still, in the day and in the dark.

But his mind wasn't still. Walter wanted something to do, something to keep a busy mind working while lying wake. He asked for a list of names to think about, to care about, to pray for. People in the parish, in the city, in the world. Walter found new work for the next months when he lay awake day or night.

Finally, Walter went back to work taking inventory, stocking shelves, meeting sales people. The work load grew.

Sleep habits, however, had changed for Walter. Now he spent more time awake in the dark; he took more hours in the night for his list of names—people to think about, for whom to pray, about whom to care. In six months of lying still, Walter had learned a skill for the rest of his life.

A prayer list is good to have at hand for restless nights.

Gladys was Walter's age. In her nineties, she went into a nursing home. At her new home, she continued what she'd done for years: Gladys sang in the night. Gladys sang and prayed in the dark. So easy was this for her to do, she soon sang in her sleep.

In the night, when I wake, I still feel the prayers of Walter and

Gladys from two distant cities, from years ago. Walter loved me, and I was on his prayer list. Gladys was my mother-in-law. Both held me safe in sleepless nights. Those prayers of the past are still a comfort.

How long does a good prayer last? Can past prayers still have power over me? I wake and I sleep inside prayers of saints. My father's prayers still hold me. My mother's folded hands are still my sacred sign for Amen.

Someone is praying for me right now.

MY WORK AND MY LIFE

My work needs to rest. I will let it sleep.

I can't get my work finished.

I lie awake tossing and turning, thinking: "I can't get all my work done. I'm running, running, running. I'm a slave to my job. My work is taking over my life."

In the night, things pile up. I see the shadow side of work, the dark side. I need to tell myself, "Keep it unfinished. See each day's work as 'to be continued,' unfinished." I need to see a day's work as open-ended. Done for the day, but not finished; the thing that keeps me moving on, into the future, down the road, over a high hill, through a valley, into a far horizon. My work continues; I'm still needed.

Work is not a dead end. Work is like a tree, growing through steps, seasons, times. The tips of each branch are green, forming, growing into twigs and buds. Work is always alive, good work is unending. It needs to be.

In the night I picture my work as a living, breathing thing. Like any living thing, work grows weary, it sleeps, it wakes to a new day.

Work has long-range goals, temporary goals, new goals. Work knows turns, milestones, setbacks. There are rest stops along the way; time to rest, recover, look around, look back, be glad, take a deep breath, look ahead.

It isn't bad to look at work as part of yourself. Work embodies our spirits, expresses our souls. It is a mirror in which we see our gifts, skills, our values, dreams, our selves. When awake in the night, several sentences help me: "I am my work. I am my work. I need sleep; my work needs sleep."

Find your own sentences: "I'm not finished, I believe my work has a long future." Or, "I don't get done because my ideas are growing." Or, "I never finish, but I have a good start." Or, "My work is like myself, it closes down at night, it reopens in the morning."

In a sleepless night, let work go to sleep. It wants to; we want it to. It needs sleep as much as we do. Wake to your work feeling like new.

My work needs to rest. I will let it sleep.

I'm stuck.

Sometimes I lie awake thinking "I'm stuck." I'm in a ditch, in a hole, buried. The work is too much, too boring. I can't make myself get going. I am not sure I can do my work anymore.

I woke thinking I lost my skill to write. Can I still play with sentences, make poems, rhyme words? It was not losing a poem or story I feared. It was losing some of myself, who I am, my gifts. When I thought about my work, I panicked; I was not sure I could do it.

I changed the picture. I climbed on top of the doubts and looked down at myself: saw the books I'd written, the hymns, the poems, the prayers. I climbed higher, looked down at my life: my goals for tomorrow, for next week, the play I'm going to write, the song lyrics I already planned, the prayer I began for my grand-daughter. These are good plans, good starts.

I can write! I'm already started. My spirit is no longer stuck. I feel high. I know I can do my work in the morning. I'll sing my way to work.

Awake at night I see my gifts, power, skills, plans; I see how I've already begun. In the dark I find the top of a hill, look at the big picture. Each night God calls me to the top of my hill. In the morning I will be ready to go down.

Some work requires climbing. If it's hard to get going and you need a fresh view, find a hilltop, a high place. From your hilltop, see who you are. Look for the end of the journey, think of your goal, the outcome. See ways in which you've already started. Keep feeling your personal mission statement.

A rabbi I know went up a high hill with his close friends. There they felt their legacy, their history, their purpose, their call. They were filled with light, glory, power. Coming down from the Mountain of Transfiguration they began a work that has not quit.

The hill gave them their running start 2,000 years ago.

In the Holy Land, pilgrims still visit high places from which to look out and get a new start in life. Shepherds' Field, Calvary, Moriah, Carmel, Olivet, Megiddo, Sinai—these are all high places. Holy hills. Find your own nighttime high place, a holy hill from which to get momentum.

Close your eyes and give thanks. Then climb to a high place, look up, look around, look down. See where you want to go. Let go. Go.

God will bring you to the top of a good hill.

I stand on a new hill with God, we look out together.

My job is too big.

I've grown to look like my job. My job is too big. I will take it apart and look at the pieces. I am bigger than my work.

I used to wake feeling I was only my job. I looked like my work, felt like my work, thought only of work. It was the mirror in which I saw myself. Fading into the background were family, fun, community, neighbors, recreation, rest. I had turned into my job. It was a nightmare.

In the night I took time to look closely at myself and my work. Was it me inside my job, or my job inside me? Which was the bigger circle, my work or myself?

I looked at the pieces of my work: skills, duties, responsibility, relationships, hours, energy, values. When I looked at my work this way, it looked like pieces of a pie; I could see what felt too big, what was too consuming.

Then I looked at myself, the circle that was me. I looked at the pieces of me: my spirit, my faith, my family, fun, friends, recreation, rest. I am bigger than my work; it was just a piece of the circle, a sliver of the whole pie. I never ate a whole pie in my life.

I had let myself become smaller than my work. I love work, but I am bigger than my job.

I played a lot when I was little, alone or side by side with friends. Play had playmates, toys, games, times, and places. Play had parts, pieces. I chose the parts I enjoyed. I ignored the others. In sleepless nights I began to think how I played with parts when little, and how I work now. Work is like play.

I have a friend whose work got too big. It wasn't the hours, the weight of responsibility, or any skills that he lacked. It was his time of life. He was big in the work world. For years, corporate leadership had required increasing excellence, effort always to stay on top. He wanted some place to begin again, at a lower rung, on the ground floor. After a heart attack and recovery, he took off a piece of his work time and changed it. Every Tuesday, rain or shine, he hammers nails, saws lumber, and works for a crew boss on Habitat for Humanity projects. Tuesday he builds houses for people who need houses. He has reapportioned his circle of hours. His circle of self is bigger than his work circle.

If the job is too big, take it apart, see what you enjoy, what takes energy, what feeds spirit, what you want to keep, what you can let go.

Every job has parts; together they are just part of a circle that makes us whole. My work is not greater than I. It has no right to keep me wake. I will have dominion over my work.

I am bigger than my work; I am more than my job.

My life seems out of balance.

When I was little, one of my favorite times was riding our country merry-go-round. But sometimes it had such a wobble that I spent most of the time running alongside it on the worn path just to keep it going.

When Mr. Sodman fixed the merry-go-round, it was better. It spun faster and longer. It was more fun. The center and the circumference had to be in sync. And it made a difference where we sat. So did our size and weight. We had to help keep the merry-go-round in balance.

Many nights I have wakened feeling I'm on a merry-go-round with a great wobble—without a solid center, with weight spread unevenly around the circumference. And I have to hop off and run alongside just to keep it going.

What are the pieces in life that balance, that make the ride more fun? In the night I think of these things. In the dark, there is time to face my life—family life, personal life, social life, spiritual life, work life.

I have four things about which I often pray to close my day, or during the times I wake in the night: my body, my mind, my spirit, my relationships. I pray about each of those things, and I pray for a good, healthy balance among them.

The center of the merry-go-round has to be solid and in sync for a good ride. The center of our country merry-go-round was set deep into cement. The circumference was the iron-and-wood platform on which we children stood or sat. We had fun at the circumference if the center was strong.

God is my center. In the night I think about that center. I see if it is still set deep and firm, if it's in sync with the rest of my life. I put my mind into the center of my circle, and think all around. I put my spirit into the center, and pray around.

When I put myself into the center the wobble goes away. The ride is smooth, fun. I sleep better; I wake better; I work better.

God is my center. I am in balance, and the ride is fun.

THOUGHTS OF AGING,
THOUGHTS OF DEATH

All the years of my life are inside me, a gift.

I'M GETTING OLDER.

I wake up again. I awake twice in one night. I have to get up like this almost every night now. I'm getting older.

What a blessing—an honor—to grow older. It's an honor to live; it's an honor to grow older.

What's older? Many grownups want to be young again. Most children want to be older. They say, "When I grow up. . . ." Passing of time is real for all ages.

A grandparent can't wait to see her grandchild each week. What does she enjoy? Watching the child grow. "I don't want to miss seeing my grandchild growing older." She is ecstatic each time she sees growth and change. Getting older is growing, a blessing, a privilege.

Growing older is passing through stages of life. Aging is living; if you live, you get to do it. Some live longer than others. My brother stopped counting at eighteen. I am seventy- two and still counting. I like my age. In the night I roll over more slowly, get up more often. But I also smile longer, think deeper. I like this growing.

What does someone growing older think about? As a child growing older, my thoughts were much the same as they are now. I remembered younger times and feelings: last year, things I didn't know, yesterday, things I learned. I was building history, learning faith. As a child I also thought of the future: what's coming next year, what's ahead tomorrow. I was building hope, learning faith.

Growing older means growing three ways—down, up, out. It's true for a tree, it's true for me. Roots grow down, branches grow up and out. I reach into the past: history, legacy; my roots go down. I reach into future: hopes, dreams; my branches go up and out. I reach for earth, I reach for heaven. I am like the great oak.

Lying awake in the dark and wishing to be young is a dead end. "If only I were younger. . . ." Which years would I skip?

HERBERT BROKERING

I stand before the mirror and stare at myself. "Subtract forty years," I say. "See what you miss? Subtract ten years, what else do you take away? Subtract five years, what is gone? Feel that wrinkle; you earned it. Touch a scar; that wound is healed. Look at those aching feet; remember hills you climbed, rocks you walked over, journeys you made."

Growing older is about more than skin and bones. Growing older is about spirit and memories and faith. I like myself in the mirror. Tonight, I have within me all of my years. Tomorrow I grow one day older, one day richer.

I know a clown who uses her wrinkles to mark face lines with makeup. Her lines are the pattern of a smile etched deep in her skin. The marks cannot be erased. Her wrinkled smile makes children glad.

I'm glad I have lived this long, continue to live. It's an honor to live, to grow older. I am certain that life is a gift that grows with the years.

All the years of my life are inside me, a gift.

Have I lost my touch?

I'm losing my touch. I don't have what it takes anymore. These thoughts keep me awake. These worries plague my sleep.

I know a man famous for his knowledge of history, for telling stories with imagination and picturesque language. Thousands loved to hear his lectures. I went to his cabin when he was old. He showed me where his life began—as a painter, sculptor, woodcarver. He imagined. He touched wood, paints, color.

As he got older he lost his touch with wood and oil paints. He kept his touch in history, research, storytelling. Did he think he lost his touch? Oh no. He multiplied it.

We touch in many ways.

Sixty years ago I held out my hand for a monarch butterfly. It was as royal a creature as I had ever held. I can still feel its touch. The butterfly told me from where it had flown, how far it would go when it left. It asked me how it felt to hold its beauty. It asked me not to put it into a jar or pin its wings to paper. When we finished meeting, the monarch flew somewhere I could not follow. It flew too high to be inside a plastic jar, too far for a wooden box.

The butterfly left its imprint on my mind. In that one touch of beauty, I am in touch with flying, with gentleness, with letting beautiful things be free, with sensitivity.

I know the feeling of touching, how something needs me, wants to be held, noticed, admired, honored, and then released to fly. I did not lose my childhood touch.

We never lose our touch. We are in touch with seasons, moods, memories, looks, persons, God.

You think you lost your touch? Look for it. See if it shows up in a different way. Touch something fragile, think about a memory. Touch a blossom so it will not notice. Look so someone doesn't see you looking. Take time to smell a bouquet, hold cut glass close, see sunshine through a jack-frost window pane. Greet a flower by its name. Show someone you care. Listen softly. Touch someone from a distance. Feel their closeness, warmth, life, spirit, faith. Be in touch with each other.

We can do this. This is God's gift of touch.

Have we lost our touch? Oh no. We once held a butterfly.

I still have my childhood touch, gentle and firm.

If I should die before I wake. . . .

I do not want to die.

My poems, lyrics, manuscripts, plays, are sometimes a race against death. They are a legacy, a memorial—a way to live on. I rise early, writing one more song, one more play, in case of death. I face death with my writing and say, "See, I am still alive."

Nevertheless, I meet death each night in the dark. Death is a door at the end of a life that has no end. I like this side of the door. I thank God for this life. I have begged for another year, month, day, for another chance. I will do most anything to live this life. What a gift, to live.

Someone told me he was not afraid to die. He had been saved, spared from death once. God had given him back his life. He called it a second chance, borrowed time. A cat has nine lives. How many lives have we?

I think of death each day, each night. Words of my childhood prayer. You know it:

> *Now I lay me down to sleep,*
> *I pray the Lord my soul to keep.*
> *If I should die before I wake,*
> *I pray the Lord my soul to take.*

I didn't like the dying part of that prayer; I always hurried to the end. Later, in my own children's prayers, I saw them race to the rest of the sentence: "I pray the Lord my soul to take." These words make the first part prayable night after night after night: "I pray the Lord my soul to take. I pray the Lord my soul to take. I pray the Lord my soul to take."

A picture in my childhood bedroom showed an angel carrying a child over a bridge into heaven. I imagined I was the child. I liked the angel; I liked being carried. This is what I imagined when I prayed, "If I should die before I wake, I pray the Lord my soul to take."

Once my mother was very sick, in a coma, at the door of death. She heard angels, saw a light tunnel, heard a voice from the other side. But she did not go through the door. Twenty years later she died before she woke; she went through the door, into the light. During those twenty years, my mother did not fear death; she knew she was going home, through a door where angels sing.

How will I die? In the dark of night I think of people of faith who have died. I am a person of faith. I want to die believing. I want to die with gusto, trusting. I want to die with imagination— walking through a river, cool, barefoot, feeling strong waves, feeling the sky, feeling good. I want to walk into the light hearing music, old songs, songs I wrote, new hymns. I want to feel the vibration of glory and light and sound the way I felt it in teenage rock studios. I want to go into a banquet hall feeling honored, a winner, victorious, hungry for good drink and good bread. I want to die the way I live—vibrating, on fire, in love.

For me, death will be like "Good night," and then "Good morning."

I believe in resurrection: my life is everlasting.

I have a terminal illness.

The doctor said, "Herbert, you have cancer." My first thought was terminal. How long do I have? That was years ago. Countless nights I lay awake, feeling and fearing the word "terminal." Where did it get this meaning for me? Emma had a different take on "terminal."

Emma was a family friend. She talked about another kind of terminal—on the underground railroad. She had been a slave. Emma loved the terminal on that railroad. Terminal meant "Grand Central Station." Terminal meant freedom. And Emma talked about heaven as her terminal, her most Grand Central Station of life.

I lie awake and think thoughts: terminal, the end, death. I look for Emma's eyes and revise: terminal, Grand Central Station, heaven, home. I need to see through Emma's eyes in the night. How are these comforting images born and grown?

Sleepless, I look west, to where Kenny and his family sleep. Thirty years ago, Kenny planted a walnut tree. He did all he could to make it grow. Why? "So my children can harvest the walnuts," he said. His children were still babies; he was planting their harvest.

Life and death play tag: the father and his children. Sometimes when I wake I borrow Kenny's eyes to reflect on terminal: the tree, harvest, children cracking walnuts—tag.

The apostle John was on the island of Patmos. Here he painted a picture of heaven—Grand Central Station. His paintings of heaven in Revelation inspire many; they inspire me. These are his pictures for life's terminal: singing, angels, praising, light, jewels. Sometimes we need John's eyes to see terminal as beauty, light, life.

In the night I look farther than I did years ago. The end is a terminal, the Grand Central Station, a tree with walnuts, a holy city of light, jewels, joy, loved ones, saints and angels, Emma and the Lord.

We wake with a terminal illness. We do not have a terminal life.

The end is the beginning. I am just beginning.

WHAT WILL HAPPEN TO THE THINGS I CHERISH?

I lie awake thinking, "My property. Everything I own. What if something happened to me? Who would get my prize possessions? Who will value what I value?"

I think of legacies I especially cherish: a dream I want to pass on, a thought I want to keep alive, a story I need to tell. Who knows the dream, the thought, the story? Who will cherish it as I do?

My will does not list my most cherished possessions. It does not mention my reasons for keeping gifts, old letters and their meaning, persons I hold close, fondest memories. How will these be passed to and kept by someone else?

I don't want to cease to exist. I believe in life after death. But how can ideas I began continue to grow, to live on after me? Who will inherit a commitment I can no longer fulfill? To whom do I will my dreams? What if I made a list of memories, stories, writings, designated for others to inherit, for others to keep alive?

In a sleepless night, make a will of good gifts for someone to inherit. Enjoy the thought of playing tag with life. Imagine someone carrying on your thoughts, your deeds, your stories, your dreams. What is a cause you believe in? How can you keep it alive by giving it to someone and saying, "You take it from here"?

Choose one person to whom you can will good things. See yourself grow beyond death, live into the future, through that person. Pick another person, add another clause to your will. Then another.

In a sleepless night make a will to hand on to others. Play tag with the future. We live in a life without end. I trust others to run with a piece of my life into their future. What I truly cherish and want to keep, I can give others in my will. It's a peaceful thought in a sleepless night.

O God, I will share my treasures; I will give dreams to others.

I NEED TO FIND THE STARS AGAIN.

Night is not a stranger. Night is becoming my friend.

I have learned to lie still for long periods in the night, looking at stars. It was not always so. For years I tossed and turned. I stared into the dark as though it were an enemy. I dreaded long night watches. I worried about years of sleepless nights ahead.

I had lost the bright stars. Staring out the window by my bed I saw many night skies. But I had lost sight of the stars.

It dawned on me one sleepless night: the stars were my childhood friends. Stars had been a world of wonder. As a child I stood under stars to dream of years ahead; stars were my wishing well.

When I was a child, the sky of stars faced heaven. Older now, I was tossing and turning, wrestling in the dark. I had lost the wishing well in the night. I decided to find and love my stars again, the distant diamonds facing heaven.

I quit tossing and turning. I walked into the dark to find the night I loved as a child. Old wishing well was overhead, stars still sometimes falling from it. I started to count, but too many new stars appeared. Night was full of stars facing heaven.

I saw old trees like new; in the dark, they had a side I didn't know, hadn't seen. A wood of ancient oaks boasted of nights it had known in its three hundred years. I heard night sounds I remembered from long ago. I saw again grass and tulips and a weeping willow in the dark. The summer night was cool upon my face.

Night became a friend that night. Why should I toss and turn against the dark? Why should I curse night watches? Sometimes when sleep won't come, visit the night you knew long ago. Get out of your bed, go outside, stand under stars and look up.

Now in my room I can see stars with my eyes closed; they are brightest when the night is darkest. And they still face heaven.

Night is my friend. Hello, Night!

☾   HERBERT BROKERING